NETFLIX

The Netflix "N" emblem

NETFLIX

ODYSSEYS

HEIDI NEWBAUER

CREATIVE EDUCATION · CREATIVE PAPERBACKS

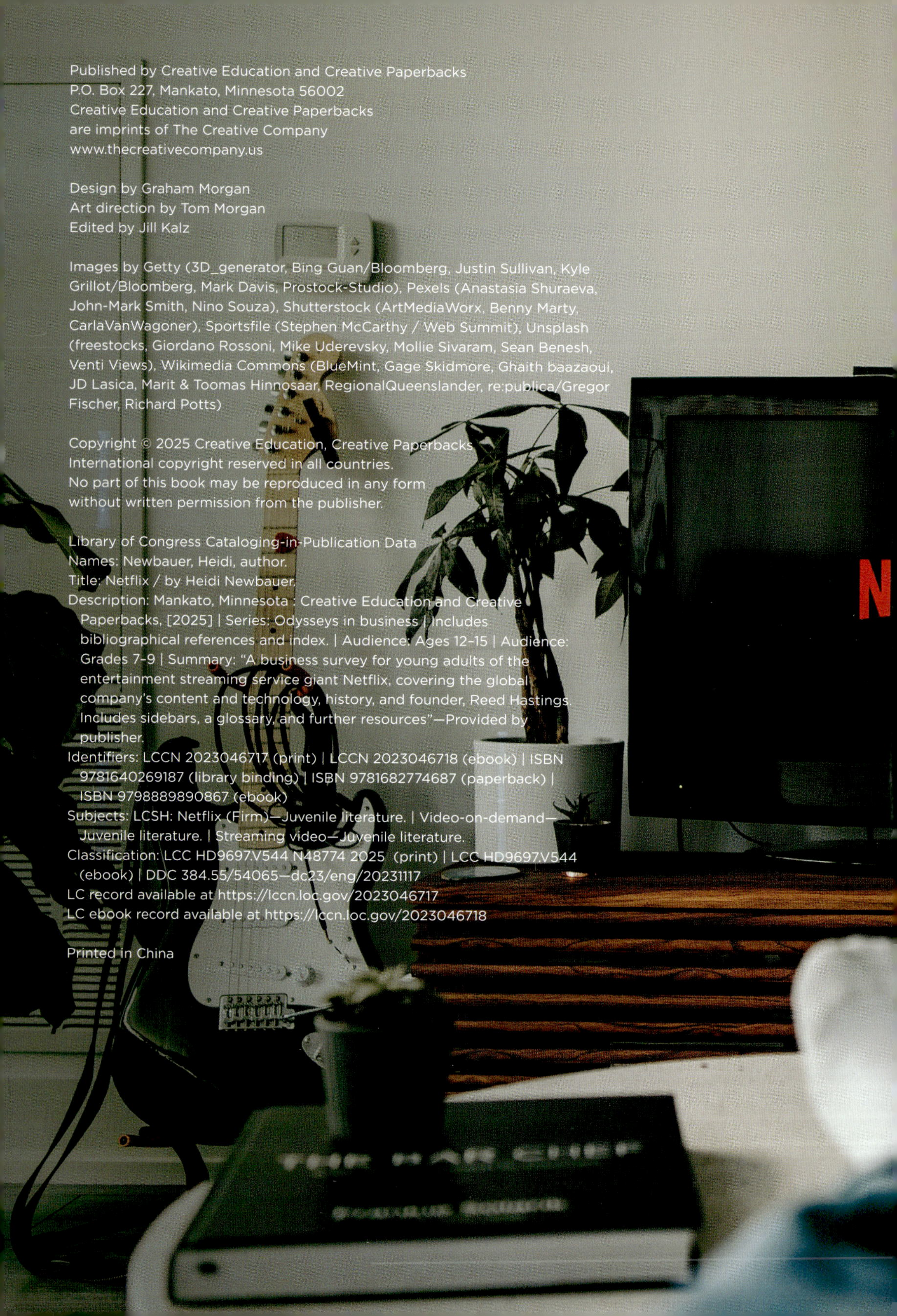

Published by Creative Education and Creative Paperbacks
P.O. Box 227, Mankato, Minnesota 56002
Creative Education and Creative Paperbacks
are imprints of The Creative Company
www.thecreativecompany.us

Design by Graham Morgan
Art direction by Tom Morgan
Edited by Jill Kalz

Images by Getty (3D_generator, Bing Guan/Bloomberg, Justin Sullivan, Kyle Grillot/Bloomberg, Mark Davis, Prostock-Studio), Pexels (Anastasia Shuraeva, John-Mark Smith, Nino Souza), Shutterstock (ArtMediaWorx, Benny Marty, CarlaVanWagoner), Sportsfile (Stephen McCarthy / Web Summit), Unsplash (freestocks, Giordano Rossoni, Mike Uderevsky, Mollie Sivaram, Sean Benesh, Venti Views), Wikimedia Commons (BlueMint, Gage Skidmore, Ghaith baazaoui, JD Lasica, Marit & Toomas Hinnosaar, RegionalQueenslander, re:publica/Gregor Fischer, Richard Potts)

Library of Congress Cataloging-in-Publication Data
Names: Newbauer, Heidi, author.
Title: Netflix / by Heidi Newbauer.
Description: Mankato, Minnesota : Creative Education and Creative Paperbacks, [2025] | Series: Odysseys in business | Includes bibliographical references and index. | Audience: Ages 12–15 | Audience: Grades 7–9 | Summary: "A business survey for young adults of the entertainment streaming service giant Netflix, covering the global company's content and technology, history, and founder, Reed Hastings. Includes sidebars, a glossary, and further resources"—Provided by publisher.
Identifiers: LCCN 2023046717 (print) | LCCN 2023046718 (ebook) | ISBN 9781640269187 (library binding) | ISBN 9781682774687 (paperback) | ISBN 9798889890867 (ebook)
Subjects: LCSH: Netflix (Firm)—Juvenile literature. | Video-on-demand—Juvenile literature. | Streaming video—Juvenile literature.
Classification: LCC HD9697.V544 N48774 2025 (print) | LCC HD9697.V544 (ebook) | DDC 384.55/54065—dc23/eng/20231117
LC record available at https://lccn.loc.gov/2023046717
LC ebook record available at https://lccn.loc.gov/2023046718

Printed in China

FLIX
ations
DARK
WHAT DO YOU
MEME?
CHAMPION

Netflix's red mailing envelopes, mid-2000s

CONTENTS

BLOCKBUSTER
VIDEO
sale
sale
WOLF CREEK 2

Introduction

The competition had an intimidating name: *Blockbuster*. The word implied greatness and strength. Something big and explosive. It was the perfect name for the video store company that numbered 9,000 stores worldwide at its peak. In the 1980s and 1990s, Blockbuster Video knew no equal.

OPPOSITE: At the height of its reign, Blockbuster had video stores around the world, from Australia to the United Kingdom, Japan to Brazil.

Other movie-rental companies, such as Family Video, Hollywood Video, and Video Place, tried to compete, but they never grew to Blockbuster's size or stamina. Then along came the little company that could: Netflix.

Established in 1997, Netflix has forever changed the way people watch videos at home. Its rise to the top has been fast and filled with risk—even a misstep or two. What started as a humble DVD-by-mail service has transformed into an entertainment giant, shipping its billionth DVD by 2007. By 2015, more than 65 million subscribers

Netflix shipped its final DVD-by-mail envelope in September 2023.

NETFLIX
EXIT

OPPOSITE Netflix users can stream thousands of hours of content with the click of a button.

worldwide enjoyed the company's streaming content, its mail-order service, or both.

Today, Netflix is woven tightly into everyday life. While it didn't create the practice of binge-watching, it's arguably the streaming service most people think of when they hear the term. In 2023, Netflix claimed more than 250 million subscribers.

Only one Blockbuster store remains.

COMEDY
COMEDY >
ACTION >
THE GOOD THIEF
GUN
GROUND CONTROL
GOOD TIME
MALONE
GUN WOMAN
HUNTED BY NIGHT
HEIST
HIGH RISK
HARSH TIMES

Push Play

It's Friday night in 2004. The coolest place to be is with your friends at Blockbuster, looking for videos to watch as your parents run to the grocery store to grab dinner. Once you and your friends pick your movies, you bring the empty **VHS** cassette boxes to the checkout counter. There, the store associate finds the videos and piles them up for you to rent for the night, or weekend, depending on the rental specials.

OPPOSITE: Video-rental stores offered all kinds of movies on VHS and, later, DVD for at-home entertainment.

This scenario was common with the rise of the VHS cassette tape and the **VCR**. For the first time, instead of going to the movie theater to see a movie, people could watch the latest film at home. All they had to do was stop at their local video-rental store and pick up a tape.

The first video store in the United States was Video Station, in Los Angeles, California. Owner George Atkinson opened it in December 1977. Soon, many of these small **mom-and-pop** businesses were springing up across the country. Eventually, businesspeople caught on to this trend, and the first video store **chain** was born: Blockbuster.

Blockbuster Video opened its first store in Dallas, Texas, in 1985. The owner, David Cook, made his store different from the mom-and-pop stores. He offered more than 8,000 movie titles, with a sophisticated, technology-based check-out process. Mom-and-pop stores usually held around 200 movies.

Additional Blockbuster stores soon opened across the country. In 1987, a few **investors** took the company even further by investing $18.5 million in it. Cook left the company later in the year, and the new management team started quickly buying out some of the mom-and-pop video stores, branding them with the Blockbuster logo. That move made Blockbuster the largest video store chain in the United States. By

1988, just a year later, 800 Blockbuster Video stores were scattered across the states.

Reed Hastings graduated with an undergraduate degree in mathematics and a graduate degree in computer science in the 1980s. He created his first company, called Pure Software (later called Pure Atria Corporation), in 1991. As his ambition for technology grew, so did his **entrepreneurial** ideas. In 1997, Hastings created the initial vision of Netflix. It's not entirely clear where the idea came from. Rumor has it that he incurred a large late fee

Netflix cofounder Reed Hastings, 2015

Netflix office in Los Angeles, California, 2022

What's in a Name?

Where did *Netflix* come from? The first part of the name, "net," is short for *Internet*. The second part, "flix," is an alternate spelling for the slang word *flicks*, meaning movies or films. The name is the perfect blend of terms related to what the company is all about. It's short, catchy, and easy to spell. Before Netflix was officially launched, it was known by those within the company as Kibble. Why Kibble? The reason was simple: Cofounder Mark Randolph already owned the Internet domain name Kibble.com.

from Blockbuster for his own movie rentals. Frustrated, he created the idea of a subscription-based movie-rental service. Regardless of whether that's true or not, Hastings was keen to see his movie-rental service come alive. DVDs were new to the market. Like VHS tapes in the 1970s, they had been introduced by Japan first, in 1995, and debuted in the United States shortly after.

Hastings's business partner in the early years of Netflix was Mark Randolph. Headquartered in Los Gatos, California, the company included Hastings,

Randolph, and eight employees. As the services of Netflix changed, so did its business culture and relationships.

Netflix started DVD-by-mail services in 1998. Initially, customers were given a seven-day rental period. By December 1999, they could pay a monthly fee to rent an unlimited number of DVDs. Considering that most rental chains, such as Blockbuster, usually charged a yearly membership fee of $50, and an average video rental cost about $5, staying at home and renting 2 DVDs for a cost of $4 each was appealing. Just a few

TAKEAWAY

Considering that most rental chains ... usually charged a yearly membership fee of $50, and an average video rental cost about $5, staying at home and renting 2 DVDs for a cost of $4 each was appealing.

months later, Netflix added the option of no late fees and a four-video monthly rental membership for $15.95. Convenience and price were in Netflix's favor.

The process was simple: A customer selected their choice of titles on the Netflix website, and up to three DVDs at a time were sent to the customer's home. After the customer watched a DVD, they sent it back to Netflix through the mail in a special pre-paid envelope. Once Netflix received

Reed Hastings and a cart full of ready-to-mail DVDs, 2002

it, their system would automatically send out the next DVD on the customer's list. This cycle continued as long as the customer was a monthly subscriber and maintained a list of titles they wanted to watch. Netflix promised to get DVDs to customers fast. Speed was a huge selling point that eventually gave Netflix the edge over Blockbuster.

Title availability also contributed to Netflix's immediate success. It had a catalog of 925 movies for viewing. *The Big Lebowski* was its most popular video rental in 1998, followed by *Office Space* in 1999.

Breaking Bad costars Bryan Cranston (*left*) and Aaron Paul (*right*)

Bad Is Good

Breaking Bad was one of the most awarded series on streaming television. It ran for 5 seasons, for a total of 62 episodes. The show received 247 award nominations from around the world. It won a total of 155 awards, including the American Film Institute's award for best series in 2014. Bryan Cranston played the role of a downtrodden, terminally ill high school chemistry teacher, Walter White. He said of his character, "I think people related to this guy. And it's never been done on television, to have a star change character during a series. And I wanted to be a part of that."

Things ran smoothly for Netflix during its early years. Hastings expanded the company's presence by securing partnerships with movie studios. He ramped up **marketing** efforts to showcase the company's catalog of documentaries, independent films, and popular series not easily available through other services.

In 2008, Netflix offered *Breaking Bad*, and the drama series became more popular on Netflix than it had been when it originally aired on television, for two reasons. First, people could watch complete seasons consecutively. They didn't have to wait a year

Netflix entertains customers in the comfort of their own homes.

for the next season. Secondly, people could watch each episode without commercials. Following the success of *Breaking Bad*, Netflix offered other shows from different studios and revolutionized how people watched them. The trend of binge-watching exploded.

Hastings also focused on quality customer service led by real people, not computers. Netflix representatives had no rules or required scripts to follow, which allowed them to personalize customer calls. For example, in 2008, a customer called in with a streaming problem.

The conversation found its way to the website Reddit, where it was praised for the integrity shown by both parties. In an interview with the *Huntington Post*, Netflix's vice president of global customer support said of the reps, "They're not restricted in any way. If somebody wants to talk to somebody in character, we encourage this."

Netflix's first decade was a good one. The DVD-by-mail system continued to do well, and customers were being entertained in a new, very convenient way. Hastings was seen as a great leader, one who was always on point. And he was—until he made a grave mistake in 2011.

At its peak, Netflix mailed DVDs through nearly 60 shipping facilities.

Netflix Culture

Reed Hastings was getting impatient. Streaming services were gaining traction in the United States, and Hastings wanted everyone to get on board. So, in 2011, he came up with Qwikster. It was a separate platform from Netflix in which people could continue to rent DVDs—but with a catch.

OPPOSITE: Reed Hastings was caught off guard by customers' negative reaction to the introduction of Qwikster.

Instead of the services of Netflix being one charge per customer, there would now be two fees: one fee for streaming services and another fee for the DVD-by-mail service. This created a 60 percent price hike for current Netflix subscribers, and the jump wasn't received well.

Many Netflix subscribers were upset. They didn't want to pay more. And they felt the divided services were more confusing than helpful. More than 700,000 people cancelled their subscription. Company stock dropped 70 percent. Netflix was sinking fast.

To try and recover some of his losses and Netflix's reputation, Hastings made an informal video of himself. In it, he explained why he wanted to implement the service changes. It was an odd move, and Hastings didn't gain any supporters.

The epic failure of Qwikster revealed that Netflix employees and **executives** were hesitant to tell Hastings if he had a lousy idea. He had been spot-on about everything else leading up to this point, but there comes a time when leadership needs honest feedback. With this mistake, a drive toward **radical transparency** at Netflix began. Being a transparent business means that information is shared with everyone in the company, from top executives to the lowest-paid positions. Hastings saw the idea of transparency as a way to change the **internal culture** of the company. It gave his employees more say in what happened in the business. However, this change put more responsibility on Netflix's employees, as well.

In addition to more transparency, Hastings knew another change was needed inside the company. He didn't want his employees to feel like they couldn't tell him that an idea was a mistake. He also wanted to encourage them to take risks. The idea of employee "freedom and responsibility" was born.

The first big test of this new freedom and responsibility came when Ted Sarandos had the opportunity to **acquire** the series *House of Cards*. Sarandos had been appointed co-chief executive officer (CEO) by Hastings in 2010. *House of Cards* would be the first series that Netflix could call "original content." The show had not run on another network or streaming service. The political drama was new and ready for acquisition.

Every network and streaming service wanted *House of Cards* as their show. The normal acquisition process was for potential buyers to see the pilot (first episode) of the show and then decide if they would buy it or not. Netflix broke this tradition. Instead of asking for the pilot, Sarandos took a chance and trusted his gut. Sarandos was a data person. He loved to analyze data, which had made him very successful in his previous job as the vice president of product and merchandising for Video City/ West Coast Video. When he moved to Netflix in 2000, he created a formula that relied on subscriber data. With this data, he made editorial decisions where "70 [percent] is the data and 30 [percent] is judgement, the 30 [percent] needs to be on top."

In March 2011, on behalf of Netflix, Sarandos bought *House of Cards* for two seasons. The cost was $100 million. Sarandos later told a reporter that he was able to do this big deal because of the "freedom and responsibility" all Netflix employees had. Not

Watch Whenever

House of Cards was Netflix's first original series. Instead of releasing the first season's episodes one at a time, Netflix released the full season all at once. Doing so gave viewers the opportunity to binge-watch all 13 episodes, revolutionizing how people watched television. Instead of recording an episode with a **DVR**, people could open Netflix on their laptop, tablet, or **smart TV** and watch episodes whenever they wanted, in whichever order they wanted. When the second season debuted in 2014, about 668,000 subscribers binge-watched the entire season in the first weekend of release.

everything needed to be run by the big boss, he said. Employees had the freedom to make decisions, but they were also responsible for those decisions, no matter the outcome. Sarandos called Hastings and told him about the deal. Hastings was excited.

The risk paid off. *House of Cards* debuted on Netflix on February 1, 2013, and was a huge success. It became the first online-only streaming series to be nominated for and win the Emmy Award for Outstanding Directing in a Drama Series. The annual Emmys are given for excellence in television, from script writing and acting to sound and costume design. In 2014, Kevin Spacey won Best Actor for his portrayal of the main character, Frank Underwood. Robin Wright won an Emmy for her portrayal of Claire, Underwood's wife. Unfortunately, sexual abuse allegations arose for Spacey in 2017, so Netflix ended their relationship with him. The sixth season of *House of Cards* aired in 2018 without Spacey.

With the success of *House of Cards*, Netflix was on a roll. Popular series such as *Unbreakable Kimmy Schmidt*, *Stranger Things*, *The Crown*, and *Squid Game* kept audiences interested and excited for more. Netflix even began producing movies. In 2018, its movie *Roma* won three Academy Awards, including Best Foreign Language Film.

The young cast members of *Stranger Things*, an award-winning Netflix sci-fi/horror original series, celebrate their success in 2017.

WATER
NETFLIX
GREY GOOSE
VODKA
MOROCCANOIL
NETFLIX
Lindt
NETFLIX

The culture of Netflix continued to expand and change. The idea of freedom and responsibility grew, as did the ideas of the Keeper Test and the Culture Deck. The Keeper Test arose from a darker time in Netflix's history, in 2001, when Hastings gathered his employees in the company parking lot, along with Chief Human Resources Executive Patty McCord. There, he announced that he was laying off one-third of the company, effective immediately. That amounted to 120 employees.

The layoffs sparked a profound change in Netflix's internal culture. The idea was that the company was a team, not a family. The layoffs were not personal. What mattered most was the good of the company. Some called the layoffs and the idea of a team cold and calculating, while others thought it was simply efficient.

Royal Expenses

One very popular Netflix series is *The Crown*, based on the life of the United Kingdom's late monarch Queen Elizabeth II. It is one of the most expensive series Netflix has ever produced. One larger expense was the recreation of Elizabeth's wedding dress in Season 1. The dress alone cost roughly $35,000. But that was only the start. Season 5, a collection of 10 episodes, is said to have cost $140 million to make. Since its debut in 2016, *The Crown* series has cost a total of $500 million!

The Keeper Test has become part of Netflix's ongoing high-expectation culture. According to the test, management has the right to critique employees for their performance. If management doesn't feel an employee is doing the best work possible, or if the employee is no longer a good fit for the position, the employee gets cut. Many people who once worked at Netflix feel that there was a culture of fear at the company. They say the objectivity of the Keeper Test could work against anyone who was having a few bad days or clashed with other employees. Yet, Netflix

Netflix headquarters in Los Gatos, California, the heart of Silicon Valley

has always believed its culture helps attract potential employees. According to the company, its turnover rate is in line with similar companies.

The Culture Deck is another key part of Netflix culture. Created by Hastings and his close colleagues, the 127-page slideshow presentation was released in 2009. At the time, Netflix was thriving in a place in California called Silicon Valley, where tech start-up companies usually begin. The Culture Deck is considered "one of the most important documents to come out of Silicon Valley" for its **innovative** ways of thinking about one's company culture. This document is said to have reinvented how human resources departments work with employees. It's been viewed more than five million times on the Internet.

Riding the Streaming Wave

Reed Hastings believes strongly in his company's internal culture. In fact, he credits it for the success of Netflix's stock price. The highest stock price to date hit on November 17, 2021, with a closing price of $691.69 per share. The high-expectation culture has worked well for the company. It has led to constant growth and trust from Wall Street investors.

OPPOSITE: Since its start, Netflix has remained mostly steady, except for the Qwikster failure and some natural ebbs and flows of the stock market.

Netflix cofounder Marc Randolph, 2017

In 1999, Marc Randolph, Hastings's business partner, stepped down as CEO, leaving that job to Hastings. Randolph spent the next couple decades in product development and left Netflix for good in 2003. Both men knew it was time to try new things. For Randolph, that meant serving as a mentor at MiddCORE and as a board member of Looker Data Sciences.

In 2012, Hastings put the Keeper Test to work with longtime executive Patty McCord. The company had grown and changed, and Hastings felt she was no longer a fit for the company. He let her go. McCord was disappointed. She had been a team member with Hastings since Netflix began. But she also understood the culture and that it was time to move on to a new adventure.

Before Netflix and other streaming services created their own original content, movies were owned by their picture corporations. For example, the movie script for the movie *E.T.* was originally bought by Universal Pictures. The film belonged solely to that studio. If a network such as NBC or a streaming service such as Netflix wanted to show *E.T.*, it would have to pay Universal Pictures to rent the film. In 2015, basking in the great success of *House of Cards,* Netflix thought it was a good time to take greater control of its content and move into Hollywood.

The Hollywood move was not just a physical move, it was also a major industry shift for Netflix. No longer a streaming start-up, the company had proven itself to be a strong player in the entertainment world. It now held a magic wand high over the land of film and television, ready to create more magic.

The Netflix headquarters in Hollywood is a movie and television lover's dream. The working campus

Video Streaming Wars

(subscribers in millions; Q3 2023 data)

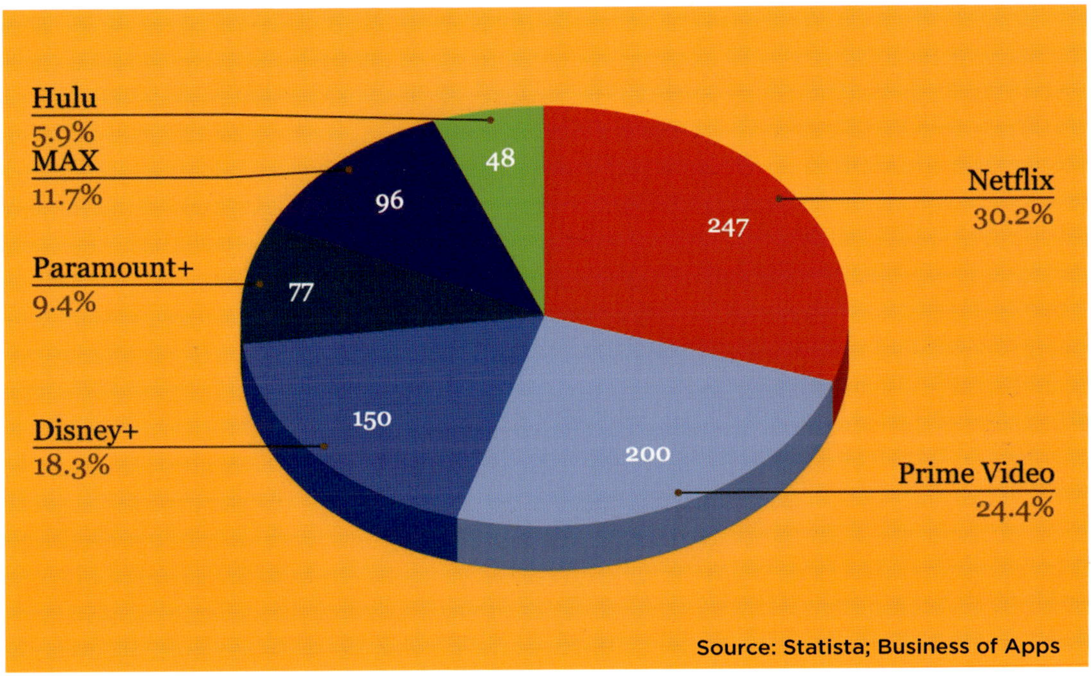

covers 3.5 acres (1.4 hectares). The tall office building with floor-to-ceiling windows offers views of downtown Los Angeles, the Griffith Observatory, and the famous Hollywood sign. Inside are large screens and sound rooms to test out original content and new technology to

Netflix opened its Hollywood office in 2018.

ensure that the output is of the best quality. Sound stages are scattered throughout the Netflix campus. They are used for filming some of the company's original content.

Being in the Hollywood spotlight has been a wonderful thing for Netflix. Being in the legal system spotlight has not. The company has faced several lawsuits through the years. In 2019, former Manhattan prosecutor Linda Fairstein filed a **copyright** lawsuit. She claimed that her character was falsely portrayed in the Netflix documentary *When They See Us*. In 2020, after the release of the Netflix original movie *Enola*

Holmes, a copyright lawsuit was filed against Netflix by the estate of Sir Arthur Conan Doyle. It claimed the company used characters created in Doyle's Sherlock Holmes series without permission, breaking copyright laws. In 2022, a shareholder lawsuit in California claimed that Netflix had not met its subscriber goals and had misled shareholders about market losses. According to the claim, Netflix wronged shareholders by "exhibiting slower [customer] acquisition growth due to, among other things, account sharing by customers and increased competition from other streaming services." As of fall 2023, the case was still open.

Netflix hasn't always been on the receiving end of lawsuits. It has filed them, too. In 2022, Netflix sued composers Abigail Barlow and Emily Bear for breaking copyright and trademark laws. The duo had created and put on a staging in Washington, D.C., of *The Unofficial Bridgerton Musical.*

TAKEAWAY

In 2020, Netflix had 204 million monthly subscribers, 54 million more than competitor Prime Video. In 2022, there were about 230 million.

Netflix believed the women copied Netflix's original *Bridgerton* series content without permission. This type of lawsuit is very common within the entertainment industry; much of what is produced is not a tangible item, such as a pair of shoes, but something that is shared through acting, dancing, or singing.

Regardless of the legal trouble Netflix has faced in recent years, it still has millions of loyal customers. In 2020, Netflix had 204 million monthly subscribers, 54 million more than competitor Prime Video. In 2022, there were about 230 million. Even with the end of the DVD-by-mail service in September 2023, Netflix was projected to soar to 251 million subscribers by 2024.

NETFLIX

Learning and Adapting

The future direction for Netflix looks promising. Even though it continues to fall short of its expected subscriber goals, the company is still a desirable pick for Wall Street investors. In the podcast *Land of the Giants*, co-hosts Peter Kafka and Rani Molla asked why Netflix can borrow more money than it makes. They pointed out that most other Hollywood and streaming-based companies do not receive that kind of special treatment.

OPPOSITE: The solid red Netflix wordmark logo debuted in 2014, representing a bold, energetic company.

Although Netflix is a global company, its service is not available in China, Crimea, North Korea, or Syria.

The answer the co-hosts got is that Wall Street likes what Netflix is doing, which is mostly showing up and innovating the market, like Jeff Bezos did with Amazon.

Netflix has subscribers in more than 190 countries and offices in 31 locations around the world. As the company has grown globally, it has learned valuable lessons and adapted. It has become much more aware of the cultural consciousness needed to thrive as an international business. What is acceptable in one country may not be acceptable in another.

In 2019, Netflix pulled an episode of a show called *Patriot Act* in Saudi Arabia. It did so because the episode contained references to the killing of U.S. journalist Jamal Khashoggi. Under Saudi Arabian law, this episode was in violation of the kingdom's anti-cybercrime law. It is a law that doesn't exist in the United States. After pulling the episode, Netflix received backlash from human rights organizations, such as Amnesty International. These organizations felt Netflix was not respecting artistic freedom and was giving in to the laws of Saudi Arabia's **authoritarian government**.

As the original content of Netflix expands, so does the company's understanding of how to do business best in different countries and different cultures. It is also continuing to learn how to best serve viewers of all types and abilities. The Americans with Disabilities

Amnesty International has fought oppression since its founding in 1961.

Act (ADA) became a law in 1990 to stop **discrimination** against people with physical or mental challenges. It works to provide needed support, such as alternate tutoring options in schools and closed-captioning services for people who are hard of hearing. Closed captioning allows viewers to read the typed transcript of a show as it happens.

In 2010, Netflix was sued by the National Association of the Deaf because it was not ADA-compliant. It did not provide the closed captioning necessary for Deaf and hard of hearing people who were streaming content. In the end, Netflix agreed to caption 100 percent of its video content by 2014 and pay about $800,000 in fines. It is now 100 percent ADA-compliant.

Showtime at the Office

At Netflix Hollywood, the walls of the 14-story office building lobby are full of liquid crystal display screens. These screens use liquid crystals to produce images, like a computer screen on a laptop or desktop, animating the latest and greatest shows of Netflix. Alongside these amazing walls of technology, the lobby holds an art installation that changes every few months. Glass cabinets hold the awards from the company's many winning shows and movies. Each area of the Netflix building is decorated in a show's theme, giving employees and visitors the feeling of being on the featured show.

Although the ban on password-sharing angered some users, Netflix saw an increase of nine million new subscribers as a result.

Keeping pace with new technology is of key importance to Netflix's future, too. Every customer must use the Netflix website, so the company has enhanced it with personalized algorithms. These instructions tailor what a customer sees based on their previous likes and dislikes. Netflix also makes sure to use the most current digitization tools possible, so subscribers have the best viewing experience.

The latest change Netflix has made is to stop password-sharing. For a long time, subscribers could share

Ted Sarandos has led Netflix's content teams since 2000 and assumed the role of co-CEO in 2023.

their passwords with other people. This allowed non-subscribers to stream Netflix for free. Netflix announced a policy change in 2022. It limited password-sharing to people living in the same household. Subscribers could add more people to their accounts outside the household for an extra $7.99 per month, or they could use a feature called "transfer profile." This feature gives a prompt to extra users to make their own, paying accounts. When asked why Netflix executives decided to make this change, a spokesperson said that while they did encourage sharing in the past, the practice was "impacting our ability to invest in great new TV and films for our members." It cost the company too much money to allow password-sharing.

The future look of streaming services, including Netflix, is a bit of a mystery. Continuous changes in technology will require companies to stay flexible and adapt quickly to those changes—or risk being left behind. Since its start in 1998, Netflix has grown a lot, and so have the people who work there. The company has been tested by unstable times, such as the failure of Qwikster, and numerous lawsuits through the years. Yet, founder Reed Hastings has stuck to his dreams and continues to believe in his company's culture, product, and employees.

In January 2023, Hastings stepped down as Netflix's co-CEO. He gave the job to Ted Sarandos and Greg Peters and assumed the

Before becoming co-CEO, Greg Peters served as Chief Operating Officer and Chief Product Officer for Netflix.

Top 10 TV Shows in the U.S. Tod

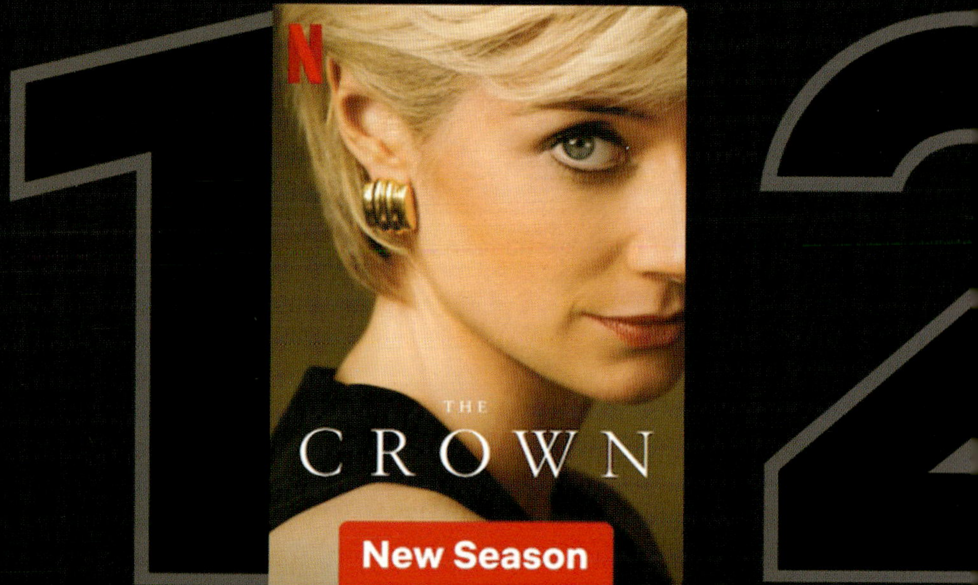

Sports TV Shows

The Netflix service not only shows users what's popular but also makes personalized recommendations.

role of executive chairman. Hastings knew it was in the best interest of the company to make a change, and so he did.

Hastings once said, "Our task is to consistently improve the quality of our service and stay two steps ahead." Netflix plans to stay innovative and grow, with its team-based company culture, original and rented content, and a passion for making at-home entertainment a fantastic, unmatched experience.

Claire Foy won a 2017 Golden Globe Award for her portrayal of Queen Elizabeth in Netflix's original historical drama *The Crown*.

Selected Bibliography

Hastings, Reed, and Erin Meyer. *No Rules Rules: Netflix and the Culture of Reinvention.* New York: Penguin Press, 2020.

Hayes, Dade, and Dawn Chmielewski. *Binge Times: Inside Hollywood's Furious Billion-Dollar Battle to Take Down Netflix.* New York: William Morrow, 2022.

Hosch, William L. "Netflix." *Encyclopedia Britannica*. September 2, 2023. https://www.britannica.com/topic/Netflix-Inc.

Kafka, Peter, and Rani Molla. "Netflix is a team, not a family." *Land of the Giants*. https://podcasts.apple.com/us/podcast/netflix-is-a-team-not-a-family/id1465767420?i=1000479218645 [Accessed June 20, 2023].

Randolph, Marc. *That Will Never Work: The Birth of Netflix and the Amazing Life of an Idea*. New York: Little, Brown and Company, 2019.

Sanders, Sam, Jinae West, and Jordana Hochman. "The Rise of Netflix." *It's Been a Minute*. August 11, 2020. https://www.npr.org/2020/08/10/900845573/the-rise-of-netflix [Accessed June 18, 2023].

Glossary

acquire to purchase or gain

authoritarian government a type of political system in which the ruler is not elected by the people of the country but usually appointed by the government

chain a group of like stores usually owned or managed by one entity

copyright the legal right to copy, display, or perform a creative work

discrimination applying different treatment to someone based on factors other than individual merit, such as race, gender, or physical ability

DVD digital video disc; a thin, round object onto which video content is burned for later playback

DVR digital video recorder; a device that can record video content to different types of electronic storage spaces, such as a disk drive, for later viewing

entrepreneurial related to a person who organizes a new business venture and assumes the risks associated with it

executive a decision-making leader of a company, such as a president or chief executive officer (CEO)

innovative original or advanced beyond the usual

internal culture a set of behaviors and beliefs that make up a team or work environment

investor someone who commits money or other resources in order to earn a financial return

marketing the promotion of products or services

mom-and-pop locally run by a single owner

radical transparency the dramatic openness of organizational processes and information throughout a company

smart TV a digital television with advanced features for streaming the Internet and streaming services such as Netflix

stock shared ownership in a company by many people who buy shares, or portions, of stock, hoping the company will make a profit and the stock value will increase

subscriber someone who receives a regularly provided product or service, usually for a fee

VCR video cassette recorder; an electronic device that can play back certain sizes of pre-recorded video cassette tapes

VHS video home system; a type of video cassette tape made for VCRs

Websites

Company Assets

https://about.netflix.com/en/company-assets
Explore photos of the Netflix office spaces.

Netflix

https://www.britannica.com/topic/Netflix-Inc
Read about Netflix's basic history and latest news.

Streaming Media

https://www.britannica.com/technology/streaming-media
Learn more about the process of streaming.

Index